GW00390845

1

Benjamin Kell was born in Andover, and grew up in Emsworth, Hampshire, UK. He studied History at the University of Plymouth, specialising in Asian History. He has travelled China extensively, and lived in Cambodia. This is his second book.

Contents

Authors' Note

There are several phrases and slang terms which appear regularly, and require clarification.

A Lady Drink is a drink bought for a bar girl. Universally priced at around $3.50, the girl usually keeps between one and two dollars. Due to low wages, this is an important source of income for the girls. It rewards those who are most confident and flirtatious, whilst those who are shy or cannot speak good English tend to get less.

A Bar Fine is the money paid to the bar to take a girl out. Often customers take a girl out for dinner or to a club, simply to enjoy their company. Considering that the customer pays for everything, this can very well be the only times some girls get to go out dancing or drinking or have an expensive meal. Other times, girls are simply taken back to the hotel.

This book derived its name from a phrase I heard cropping up in conversations on a fairly regular basis. It is given as friendly advice, in addition to an arm around the shoulders, to girls who feel overwhelmed with what they have to face. When confronted with so many trials and setbacks, and with such a limited arsenal at their disposal, it isn't surprising that many of these girls turn away from their problems and try 'not to think too much.'

Acknowledgments

First of all I would like to thank each and every girl who spoke with me. Some opened right up, telling me their deepest and darkest secrets, reliving, for my benefit, stories of death and rape and loneliness. Each of these girls agreed to speak with me in order to share their story with the world, so that people can understand the real lives these girls have to live, and to dispel the stereotype of sex-hungry Asian girls who sleep with any man who looks at them for enjoyment as largely fictitious.

I would also like to thank my family, who always tolerated my frequent flights, my incessant reading and the subsequent carpet of books, and my inability to hold down a steady job. My two sisters campaign for women's rights in the UK, and I hope this book will do them proud.

DON'T THINK TOO MUCH

A study on the lives and situations of bar girls in Cambodia in the cities of Phnom Penh and Kampong Som.

Methodology

To come into contact with these girls I used several approaches. As a rule, these girls are very friendly and approachable; it pays to be so. It is in their interests to placate the customer as much as possible to ensure a maximum number of lady drinks and a good tip. However, this friendliness often terminates as things get more personal. When speaking to many girls I was often rebuked, viewed with suspicion and mistrust. Most customers don't really care about their backgrounds, and for me to pull out a notepad was viewed, not without reason, with scepticism. Many of these girls are unable to read or write, and for me to start scribbling away in a language utterly alien to them made some a bit wary. I therefore adapted my methods. One such way I approached it was to use my friends; several of them worked in bars. They knew my curiosity was entirely innocent, and I had discussed the idea with them before embarking on it. I would often sit with them, perhaps bringing with me sliced mango or fried snacks. For the most part, my friends were sympathetic to my cause and happy to help. However, I still wished to source other interviewees. This involved building a rapport with girls in different bars. My previous methods unsound, I decided to spend time with the girls and build a relationship based on mutual respect. I would often bring snacks or playing cards with me, and would only ask about interviews well after we became comfortable with one another.

I also tried my utmost to keep the interviews informal. Most of the topics covered are what the girls discuss with customers on a daily basis: family, work, home country. Listed below are the issues I wished to cover; rather than rigorously asking each and every question directly I would simply steer the conversation the way I wanted it to go. Don't think of them as questions answered, rather as areas covered.

Premise

I decided to write this book for two reasons: one personal and one academic. The first reason is that I felt horrified with what I witnessed and I wanted to do something about it. Their lives are pretty taboo, and most institutions stay well clear. The only involvement of any kind of institute I saw actually in the bars themselves was a foreign-run NGO which distributed condoms. Initiatives helping girls leave the trade and learn new skills exist but are oversubscribed and cannot promise the monetary returns prostitution can. Asides from that, I never saw any kind of police or security system protecting the girls from overly lecherous or violent customers. More on that is covered in the interviews.

The second reason is that there are very few publications which offer these girls a platform. I felt these girls needed to be able to share their stories, to educate people so that they know the truth about the trade which most people simply accept as being normal in developing countries. Some books actually make out that the trade is glamorous, and are little more than guidebooks for whoring. Others are full of analysis and evaluation proffered by Western educated academics or sociologists. To these girls, it is much simpler; sex equals money which equals food. I wanted to write a book where, although 'steered' by me, these girls will be able to air their grievances and express themselves freely, and their answers to be published without alteration or censor.

Criteria

The criteria for this book was quite simple; the candidate had to be, or had to have been, a bar girl. There are obviously many other sources I could have used for this area of research; other academics or specialists who have covered this before, or the *tuk tuk* drivers who take the girls and their clients to hotels, or the shop assistants who sell condoms and lubrication to impatient men as a girl/s wait in the *tuk tuk* outside. All these people would have provided fascinating insights, but I felt that only the girls in the trade themselves would be able to tell me what it is really like. Only they could tell me their reasons for choosing to work in bars, their reasons for going home with customers (or not) and how they feel about not only their job but also themselves.

Questions and Answers

The questions I have chosen to ask have been designed to allow the interviewee the freedom to navigate their own thoughts, and to share with me what they wish to share. The questions also allow for digressions and

16

offshoots, which have been included. They allow for each interview to show us a slightly different side of the bar trade, from a slightly different angle, and for the personality and individuality of each girl to come through.

Background

Things like age and hometown are important when considering the demographic of the workers; are they predominantly young, suggesting that this may be their first choice of work, or are they older, suggesting they have been working other jobs? And are they local, living close to the Riverside, or have they come from distant, poorer provinces? People from Phnom Penh are, on average, more skilled and better educated than their rural counterparts; is this reflected in the interviews?

Family

Family can be a decisive factor for girls working in bars. Do they have a large family to support? Are members of their family ill or in education, needing financial support? Or, on the flip side, do they have no family? With no one to support them or give emotional support, have they come to find work because they have nowhere else to go?

Work

Finding out about their work experience is important for understanding how bars are viewed by the women who work there. Is it their first job, or their last resort? Finding out why they chose to work in a bar, over the marketplace or in a factory, also gives insight into how these girls view themselves and where they wish to go.

Education

Just as in every society, education is a strong factor in determining where people end up spending their lives. But in developing countries, where money is hard to come by and connections can mean more than qualifications, the young are forced to study tirelessly if they wish to escape the poverty cycle. Speaking English is essential in Cambodia, and its nightlife is no exception. Those who can speak English have more choices in life, yet some still work in bars. Finding out why is essential to debunking the myth of bar girls all being uneducated and rural.

Sex

Not all bar girls are prostitutes, and not all prostitutes are bar girls. The decision to sleep with customers is an individual one; I have yet to meet a girl who has been forced into it by her manager or likewise. That said, sex is much more openly discussed and acknowledged in these circles; the taboo certainly doesn't exist in these places. For this reason, finding out why a girl *doesn't* go home, with so many of her friends sporting the monetary returns of doing so, can be just as enlightening as finding out why some do.

Reactions

This is perhaps the most important question. It shows how the older generation reacts to the idea of their daughter or granddaughter working in a very undesirable trade. It shows a lot about the role of the family in Khmer culture. How the girls react to their family's views is also insightful; how does the girl view her family, and what importance does she place on their views and wishes?

Future

These girls come to bars from many different parts of Cambodia for many different reasons; one thing they nearly all have in common is that they don't want to stay in bars forever. Knowing what they wish to do in the future is important; some wish to marry a foreigner or learn English, and both of these targets are made much easier to attain when working in a bar. Others want to start their own business, and are just working for the money. It is important to know what these girls wish to do when they leave, and how they wish to achieve it.

Introduction

Between June 2014 and April 2015 I lived in Cambodia.

One long weekend, taking advantage of one of the many Khmer bank holidays and lax road safety laws, I rented the biggest motorbike I could afford and set off around *Tonle Sap,* the great lake in the centre of Cambodia. I went anti-clockwise, from Phnom Penh to Scuon and Siem Reap and returning via Sisophon and Pursat. Returning earlier than scheduled, I decided to be a tourist for the night; my day to day work required formal attire and a professional attitude, and I was keen to cast these off as I entered the famous Riverside area. Donned in shorts and a t-shirt, I made my way through the tourists and *tuk tuk* drivers and settled down at a bar. Immediately a young lady sat down next to me and, in broken English, asked how I was. I replied in Khmer, much to her astonishment, and we continued to speak in her mother tongue. Indeed, it transpired that the limit of her English was the sentence which she had already used and vocabulary useful for working in a bar, such as 'Drink', 'Play pool' etc. We soon became good friends.

To say that she intrigued me is an understatement. Her entire life was the complete opposite of mine; unfortunately, what with my young life having been very happy, this meant that hers was one full of struggle and want. As we got to know each other, I found out more and more about her and was in a constant state of awe at her ability to persevere. When she was ten, her parents divorced after a long and unhappy marriage. She was left with her father and four siblings. When she was thirteen, her father was injured at work and she had to leave school and work so that her younger siblings could go to school. She confessed that she has slaughtered 'many, many' chickens for market. At fifteen she left Cambodia for Thailand, and worked illegally with her mother selling shoes. All the money she earned was sent back to her father. After returning to Cambodia she moved to Phnom Penh alone, and worked as a cleaner and a cook for a family, where she was raped, losing her innocence to her boss. Without the contacts or money to file a police report she upped and left, terrified of his bad temper. She got a job as a bar girl, and has worked there ever since.

The only thing that shocked and appalled me more than the suffering she had endured was the reactions I received from colleagues and friends. My manager was a French-Khmer; ethnically Khmer, she had lived in Paris since the age of two. When I told her I had met someone who worked in a bar, she furrowed her brows. 'They're not good, those girls. They're after money. Be careful, she won't let you leave. All the girls who work in bars are trying to find a Western husband, they're all like that. Why don't you look for a nice girl from here [in the local village]?' Her husband, a Khmer national, was much the same: 'Wow, a bar girl? Ha ha, why do all foreigners like bar girls? Don't tell her when you're about to leave, she won't let you. You'll have to pay her off or she'll accuse you of rape or something. Make sure you don't meet her parents… Marriage is pronounced *reap gah;* if you hear her say that, just leave, ok?' Needless to say, I was confused. I was sure that she was genuine. I consider myself a pretty good judge of character, and I was certain she wasn't lying. When recalling her rape, she cried. But on the other hand, my boss and her husband had a much deeper knowledge of Cambodia than I, and in some aspects they were right. It is not uncommon to see a Khmer woman with a Western man twenty or thirty or forty years her senior. Soon after this episode, I went to meet a Khmer drinking friend. Completely uneducated, he is a world away from the Khmer I was accustomed to meeting professionally. I ran my predicament past him. 'You're stupid! The girls who work in bars are no good!' I enquired as to why, justifying myself as best I could. He cut across: 'The girls who work in bars like money. They like foreign men because foreigners have money'. We both drank deeply, and he laughed loudly and slapped my thigh. I mused for a little while longer, as he gave me a friendly, yet searching stare. This wasn't something I could come to a conclusion over in a few minutes. I decided to give the issue more thought at another time.

It was then I decided to delve deeper into the matter. To tar all these girls with the same brush is nothing short of stupidity. But I can testify that to some of the girls who work in bars in the tourist areas a Western husband is the ultimate prize. I would need to speak to more girls.

Prologue

Whilst researching this book I met some very strange people, and found myself in some very surreal situations. The following three I think will be of most interest to you, the reader. They help to explain my drive to conduct this project, and some of the obstacles I was up against.

One night, I was playing cards in a bar. I taught some of the girls to play Go Fish, and we often whiled the evening away in such fashion. On this particular night, all heads suddenly spun round when the door was thrown open with such force that it slammed into the wall. To the complete surprise of the girls, as well as myself and the two other customers, a Khmer man stormed in and struck one of the girls across the face. She covered her face with her hands, and he grabbed her hair and pulled her off her chair. I sprang to my feet, rushed over and shouted in Khmer 'Don't hit her!' His wild eyes found mine and he screamed, mad with rage 'She's my wife!' 'I don't care!' I roared back 'Don't hit her!' Before I could do anything else, I felt hands grab my arms and shoulders from behind as the girls I was playing cards with pulled me back to my seat. 'Don't fight him' they said. 'That's her husband. Don't get involved.' Pushed back into my seat, I watched as he dragged her outside. 'That isn't right' I said to the girls I was with. 'It doesn't matter if he is her husband, he shouldn't hit her'. One of the girls looked away, ashamed. 'I know. Khmer men aren't good men.' The girls left me to comfort their friend, and I felt it wisest to stay where I was. My anger turned upon the two other customers, who said and did nothing during the whole affair. One of them took a drag from his cigarette and looked at me: 'How would you feel if your wife worked here? Let 'im get on with it. You see the girls here, the barman, they don't get involved. It's her problem'. 'That still doesn't give him the right to hit her like that. He's the husband, he's supposed to provide for her. If he doesn't, can you blame her for finding work?' The customer shrugged. 'And', I continued 'if he's happy to beat her like that in front of all these people, imagine what he will do when they're home. He's going to fucking kill her'. The customer pulled a face of indifference. 'Not my business', he said.

Another time, I was in a bar I would visit quite frequently. One of the ladies walked out, closely followed by a rather fat man. I looked away, as they tend to be bashful if I watch them flirt their way into the back of a *tuk tuk* and to a hotel. 'She's hot, but a bit pricey'. I looked up, and found the fat man talking to me in an Australian accent. 'She's charging $50,' he said, answering a question I didn't ask. 'If it was busy and there were lots of guys, $50 is ok. But it's quiet, I wouldn't give her more than $30 tonight. And she's not exactly young, is she?' I looked at the girl in question. Unable to understand a word, she smiled serenely and glanced between the two of us, trying to look as beautiful as possible with the hope he might change his mind and take her to a hotel. He didn't

26

know I knew her; I knew that she works at the market as well, totalling nearly twenty hours a day. I knew that her two children were asleep at home, waiting for their mother to come home and make breakfast, oblivious to the fact that she sells herself to buy the food she puts on that table. 'I mean, I would fuck her' he continued, 'but I'm pretty knackered anyway. And $50 is $50.' He sat down and proceeded to tell me, in detail, about his sexual achievements in Cambodia. 'They're fucking great, these girls. Threesomes, anal, whatever you want. And so cheap, much cheaper than Thailand. Just make sure you wrap up, you know what I mean?' This went on for some time. He eventually left, alone. Once he had gone, the lady turned to me. 'What did he say?' She asked. 'You looked at me when you spoke'. I smiled a hollow smile. 'Nothing', I said. 'Nothing important'.

Another night at that bar I arrived to find my friend (mentioned in the *Introduction*) in high spirits; I went to greet her, but she told me not to. 'I'm with a customer', she said. 'If you hug me, he will think we are close and he won't tip me'. I proceeded to go to the bar for a drink. 'Hello mate, how are ya doin'? Do you know this girl then?' He gestured to my friend. 'A bit, I come here a lot, I know most of them'. He grinned. 'I'd fuck her. But she's so dark. Why are you so dark?' He directed the question at my friend, who smiled, unable to understand. 'I mean, you know, she's fit and whatever, but too dark. There are fitter girls here. Don't get me wrong, I'd take her home, but I'd rather get another girl'. I remained silent, smiled, and retreated with my beer. After he had left, my friend returned to me, clutching three dollars. She asked what he had said about her, and I replied it wasn't of importance. She narrowed her eyes, and implored that I tell her. 'He said you were too dark. He'd like to sleep with you, but you are too dark and he'd rather sleep with someone else'. Her face fell, and I apologised. She laid the money on the table. 'It doesn't matter. How rude'. 'Sorry', I replied.

Banteay Meanchey

This interview was conducted in Phnom Penh, 24th November 2014.

I explained my motives to the interviewee and she agreed to answer any questions I may have.

Interview conducted in Khmer.

So, what is your name?

My name is Vantha.

Where are you from?

I am from Sisophon, which is north of Siem Reap. Banteay Meanchey province. It is very nice there, but very poor. When I was small I used to play with the other children, and my brothers and sisters. We used to ride the buffalo through the rice fields. I was very happy as a child.

I see. And how old are you?

I am twenty-four, but will be twenty-five in a few days.

Could you tell me about your family?

Sure. I am one of six; I am number three. My mum and dad have split up, and my mum lives in Thailand. I used to live with her; I can speak Thai by the way! So my mum and my older sister live in Thailand, and my dad and my other brothers and sisters live in Sisophon.

So you came to Phnom Penh alone?

Yes. I came here to work, four years ago. I worked as a housemaid; I washed the clothes, the dishes, the floors. It was very hard work, but the pay was ok and I could send money home. Every day I would go to the market, and I slept very little. But I was happy, I liked my boss...

Why did you leave?

The boss's husband raped me.

You don't have to tell me, it isn't a problem.

No, it doesn't matter. I want to tell you... He was a French man, and his wife was Khmer. When she was out he raped me. He was very strong, and very big. He was very fat and I am very small [Vantha barely reaches five foot]. Afterward I demanded money from him, but he said that I had enjoyed it...

[The interview was paused to allow time for Vantha to compose herself]

He didn't give me anything. He took my virginity and gave me nothing. I went to the doctors where I did a blood test for HIV, which came back negative. I had no choice but to leave. He threatened me, and said if I tell his wife or the police he would make my life very difficult.

I see. Thank you for telling me this. I want to ask you, why did you ask for money?

Because now I am not original! I cannot get married now, people will think I was a prostitute! At least if he gave me money I could send it home to my brothers and sisters. Instead he gave nothing and took my virginity.

Thank you for telling me this.

It is the truth, it happened. You should know.

Before you came to Phnom Penh, did you go to school?

Um, yes, for some time. But my father had an accident when I was fourteen, and I had to stop. He fell off a ladder and hurt his leg. He couldn't work, and this was after my parents had broken up, so we had no money. I left school and worked slaughtering chickens for market so that my little brothers and sisters could continue studying. This is why I can't speak English.

But you can speak Thai?

Yes, just Thai and Khmer. But Thai people don't like Khmer people working in their country. I would rather know English!

I see. So how long have you worked in the bar?

32

About six months or so. Six days a week, twelve hours a night.

Do you like it?

No. People assume I'm no good, but I need the money. I have to support my family; my father still doesn't work much, they still need more money.

Why did you choose to work in a bar? Why not elsewhere?

Because I don't have a choice. I don't speak English. I can cook, but only Khmer food. Cooking Khmer food brings in a small salary. And I can clean, but it is very tiring. Long shifts carrying sheets and mopping. Here I can sit down and relax, and I can get tips too. I don't get many, but I do get some.

What is your salary here?

$120 per month, plus tips. But my rent is $60 and anything I have left over after food and bills I send home.

I see. Does your family know you work in a bar?

No. I haven't told them. I hate to lie to them, but if I tell them they would be so ashamed. My mother always tells me to go and work in Thailand with her, but I don't want to. She has my older sister with her, she doesn't need me there too. I need to earn money on my own, not take any from my mother.

Do you go home with customers?

No, I do not.

Why not?

I don't want to. I hate it when customers touch me. I always tell them not to, but some do [anyway]. But if I don't let them touch me they don't give me tips.

[Interview is paused again whilst Vantha composes herself]

I don't want to go home with them, I refuse to. But it means I have less money than other girls. It is so hard.

I understand. I have one more question, is that ok?

Yes, ask me.

What do you want to do after you leave the bar?

I don't know. I love to cook, and I am really good at cooking. Maybe open a restaurant or something. But now I must save money for my family.

Vantha, thank you very much. You have told me many things.

No problem.

Battambang

This interview was conducted in Phnom Penh, 16th March 2015.

I explained my motives to the interviewee and she agreed to answer any questions I may have.

Interview conducted in Khmer.

So, what is your name?

My name is Srey Oun.

Where are you from Srey Oun?

I am from Battambang. It is very beautiful. It has many French houses from before the war. My family used to live near those buildings. My father was well-known as being a kind man, and educated. He would often help people.

Yes, I have been there, I like it there. How old are you Srey Oun?

I am thirty-five.

When did you come to Phnom Penh?

I came here three years ago, when my parents died. They both died in a traffic accident. I felt I had nothing there, but many relatives came to ask for money and possessions. I couldn't stay. I came here with my little boy.

Oh, you have a child?

Yes, I used to be married. To a Khmer man. But he wasn't good. He used to hit me and he had many girls. He was like a butterfly, always finding other girls. I broke up with him and came here.

And you live alone?

Yes, with my little boy. He is just three. He is at home now, near Diamond Island. It is not far from here. I have a moped and come here on my own.

I see. And have you always worked in bars?

No, I have only worked here for five months. I used to work in a factory, making clothes. At first I had some money from my family, but when I had spent it I had to work. I was there for about one year. But I didn't like it. It was exhausting, and the pay wasn't very good.

How much?

It was just $120 per month. Here I am on $150. But I have to help the cashier too, do the paperwork. But I can get tips and lady drinks too. And sometimes, maybe when my baby is sick, I can go with customers.

I don't like it, but when I really need the money I have no choice.

I see. Do you have brothers and sisters?

Yes, I do. I have two brothers and two sisters. They are all still in Battambang. They have families there. They still have people in Battambang. But because I am divorced I don't, so I moved here.

Do they know you work in a bar?

They don't know I work here, I haven't told them. They don't need to know. They would think I am stupid, you know. I am old. I am thirty-five. And I have a baby! Most of the girls here are just twenty or twenty-five. And I can only speak a little bit of English.

I understand. What do you want to do when you stop working here?

I don't know yet. It is hard; factory or bar. I am not beautiful, and I cannot speak English. It is hard for me to find another job, a better job.

Srey Oun, thank you for talking to me. I really appreciate it.

No problem. See you later.

Kampong Cham

This interview was conducted in Phnom Penh, 5th March 2015.

I explained my motives to the interviewee and she agreed to answer any questions I may have.

Interview conducted in Khmer and English.

So, what is your name?

My name is Na Van.

How old are you?

I am twenty-three years old.

Where are you from?

I am from Kampong Cham province.

When did you come to Phnom Penh?

Um, when I was sixteen so… Seven years ago.

Did you come to work or study?

To work.

And what did you do for work?

I made clothes, in a factory. I used the sewing machine to stich t-shirts.

I see. Did you come with friends or family, or alone?

I came alone. But now my older brother and both my parents have moved here too.

What languages can you speak? Did you go to school when you were younger?

I went to school for six years when I was young. I learnt English there, but not much. I have learnt to speak more English since I have been working in a bar, as many of the customers are English-speaking. I used to play too much, and not always listen. If I had listened I would be able to speak more now. Also, the teacher was poor.

How long have you worked in bars?

I have worked in bars for three years now. So four years or so in the factory, and now three years here.

Why did you choose to work in a bar?

I had to, I needed the money to support the baby.

Sorry, I didn't realise you have a baby!

No, not my baby, my brother's. He has a seven-year-old son, and I help to support him.

Does your family know you work in a bar?

No, they do not. But I have a British boyfriend, who I met here. My family have met him. I told them I met him in a restaurant. I don't think they would be happy if they knew. People think that girls who work in bars are bad girls.

Do you like working here?

It is ok. Better than when I was making clothes! That was a horrible job. So exhausting and dull. But the money is the same, $120 per month. But here I get tips and lady drinks too. That is very useful. Although now I have a boyfriend I don't need those so much.

I see. What do you wish to do after you stop working here?

I don't know. My boyfriend wants to support me, but his salary isn't very good. Better than mine, but still poor. I can't stop working. I hope, one day, that he will earn more and be able to support me. I could stay at home and take care of the house or cook food. I love to cook.

Na Van, thank you very much.

No problem! I think this is a good thing to research. People should know what it is like for us.

This interview was conducted in Phnom Penh, 21ˢᵗ March 2015.

I explained my motives to the interviewee and she agreed to answer any questions I may have.

Interview conducted in Khmer.

So, what is your name?

My name is Panha.

Where are you from?

I am from Kampong Cham.

How old are you?

I am twenty-eight years old.

Tell me about your family.

My mum is still alive, and is in Kampong Cham. My father has died...

Sorry, how did he die?

He was sick.

My condolences. Please continue.

I have two older sisters and two older brothers. One of my sisters is in Kampong Cham, and the other is here, in Phnom Penh.

What about your brothers?

One is in Kampong Som, the other is in Siem Reap. They both do labouring on building sites. The pay is very poor, but it is straightforward work. Exhausting but simple.

Do you have any children?

I don't, but my sister does. I live with her. It is very difficult. I work nights and during the day the baby is crying or playing. It means I never get proper sleep. Look at my eyes, I am so tired all the time! You know, we used to be able to sleep here. The manager didn't mind if we slept on the sofas when we weren't busy. But customers complained, saying the girls here are lazy and don't care. So now we can't.

I see what you mean. Does your sister work?

No, she stays at home to take care of the house and care for her child.

What languages can you speak?

I speak a little bit of English, and Khmer, of course. When I studied I had little money. I couldn't afford to study English further. I only studied a little bit. I used to study in a pagoda. It was 500R per hour [12.5 US cents].

Can you read and write Khmer?

A little.

Are you married?

No, not yet. I used to have a boyfriend, but we have since broken up.

Was he Khmer or foreign?

He was Khmer.

I see. Why did you break up?

He has money, and I don't. He wanted a girlfriend with money, with an education.

So, he broke up with you?

Yes.

Was this in Kampong Cham?

Yes, it was. But he is in Phnom Penh now.

But you don't have any contact with him?

No, I don't. I don't want to speak to him. And he doesn't know where I live, or where I work. Maybe he would try to meet me for sex. He just wants sex.

I see. How long have you been working in bars?

Five months.

Do you like it here?

No, I don't. But I have no money. When I have money I send it to my older sister. She is living in Africa. She married an African man. They have no money.

Sorry, where is she? Which country?

In Africa.

I see. Does she work there?

No, she must care for her child and take care of the house. She has married an African man, and he cares for her and earns the money.

I see. I wish to ask, do you sleep with customers?

I used to. I still go with one particular man. When I have no money, I have no money. Those men were British and American.

What about this man you still sleep with?

He is old, sixty I think. I don't know where he is from. He is friends with the owner. I like older men, they're easier. Fifty or sixty years old is good.

Sorry, what do you mean by 'easier'?

They have no energy. They are easier to deal with [in the bedroom].

Oh, I see. Thank you for telling me this. Does your family know that you work here?

They know I work here, but they don't know I sleep with customers. They don't know… My brothers don't know…

I see. What would they think if they knew?

They would think very badly of me.

Thank you. What did you used to do for work before this?

I worked for a Chinese company. I was a greeter. I had to *sompeah* customers.

How much do you earn here, in the bar?

$100 per month.

And you get tips, yes?

Yes. Sometimes, just one or two dollars, sometimes five or ten or twenty dollars.

How much do you work?

I work eleven hours a night, with two days off a month.

What do you want to do when you leave this place?

I want to sell food, to cook and sell food, snacks. I like to cook. You know on the street, ladies who sell noodles or rice or bread? Like that.

Are you looking for a new boyfriend?

Yes, but I haven't met a nice boy yet. It is impossible to find a nice boy working in a bar. Khmer or foreign, I don't mind. If they have a good heart, that is good enough.

Thank you very much. Do you have anything else to add?

My ex-boyfriend is now married. His wife speaks and writes English, the same as him. She has money; I do not. If you understand English you have options. I don't, so I don't.

Panha, thank you so much.

My pleasure. Oh, one last thing. I am not really twenty-eight years old.

No? What then?

I am thirty-five.

I see. Why did you say you were twenty-eight?

Because thirty-five is old! If the boss knew I was that old, maybe he wouldn't have me work here. Or I'd work behind the bar, where I wouldn't get tips. I don't want anyone else to know.

I see. Well, thank you very much.

No problem!

This interview was conducted in Phnom Penh, 20ˢᵗ March 2015.

I explained my motives to the interviewee and she agreed to answer any questions I may have.

Interview conducted in Khmer.

So, what is your name?

My name is Srey Sor.

And where are you from?

I am from Kampong Cham. It is not that far from here, just one hour, an hour and a half. I am from Scuon. Do you know it?

Yes, I have been there. People there eat spiders, yeah?

Ha ha yes! They are delicious!

How long have you been here?

Not long. A few weeks.

Do you have a family?

Yes, I do. They are in Kampong Cham. My mother and father and siblings. My children live with my parents. I work too much.

So you were married?

Yes, I was. To a Khmer man. I got married with him when I was quite young, when I was twenty. Now I am twenty-eight. My parents agreed he was a good match, and we got married. I had to do as they said. It was not a good marriage. We have divorced, but I have the children. They stay with my parents, who look after them. One girl and one boy. They are very cute!

Why did you divorce?

He chased other girls. He was sleeping with other girls. I stopped loving him. He was not a good man.

I see. Why did you choose to work here?

In Phnom Penh?

I mean in a bar.

There are no jobs in Kampong Cham. It is very difficult. So I came here. There are some factories [in Kampong Cham], but not many. And the pay there is less than here.

But why did you choose to work in a bar?

I don't have a choice. I cannot speak English, so there are few jobs for me. And I don't want to work in a factory. Factories are hot and exhausting.

Do you like it here?

[Srey Sor paused]

No, I don't.

Why not?

It is horrible. I cannot speak English. Just Khmer. And many customers here can just speak English. So they don't sit with me. They don't give me tips or buy me drinks. Some just want to touch me. I sit with them because I have to, and they try and kiss me or touch me, touch my leg. And I cannot tell them to stop, because I cannot speak English. But if I move away, they won't give me a tip. I refuse to go home with them. I have only ever had sex with my ex-husband. We were married. I cannot have sex with a man I do not know. I just cannot.

I see. I am sorry.

But I have no choice. I have to look after my children. I have to work hard and send money home to them. I cannot stop work or find other work. I have to send money home every month. I must think of them, not of myself.

Yes. So, what do you want to do after you stop working here?

I don't know yet. I want to be with my children. I want to save money and go back to them. Or rent a house and bring them here. But I really don't know. It will be a long time yet. If I find a decent man then I won't have to work. I can see my children and cook and care for the house.

Srey Sor, thank you for talking to me.

It is ok. Good luck [with the book].

49

Kampong Chhnang

This interview was conducted in Phnom Penh, 17th March 2015.

I explained my motives to the interviewee and she agreed to answer any questions I may have.

Interview conducted in Khmer.

What is your name?

My name is Dai.

How old are you?

I am thirty-four.

Where are you from?

Kampong Chhnang.

Did you go to school?

I did, but not for long. I have no dad, so I didn't have much money. He left before I was born. Education is expensive.

Did you ever study English?

No. I wanted to, and still do, but I don't have the money.

I see. Do you have any brothers or sisters?

I have an older sister

When did you move from Kampong Chhnang to Phnom Penh?

I came when I was eighteen.

What did you do when you first came?

I worked in a factory, making clothes.

How much did you earn in one month?

Just $45.

Wow, that is so little!

Yes, I know…

Did you come with your family, or on your own?

I came with a friend, and we both worked in the same factory.

Why did you leave Kampong Chhnang for Phnom Penh?

Back then, there were no factories in Kampong Chhnang. There was no work to be had. We both came because we knew there were more jobs in the city, and foreigners. Foreigners have money.

Where is your family?

My mother is in Kampong Chhnang. My father left her when she was pregnant with me; I have never met him. I know he was in the army, and was based in Pursat, but apart from that I know nothing about him.

Do you have any children?

Yes, three: two boys and one girl.

Do you have a husband?

I did, but we broke up. I left him one year ago.

Was he Khmer?

Yes, he was. He was a bad husband. Lazy, he didn't work... drank a bit, but smoked a lot. I finished it, it was my decision. I couldn't tolerate him anymore.

So you are single now?

Yes.

Are you looking for a new man?

Yes! I want to find an American, and go to live in the US.

How much do you earn in one month here?

$120. I work six nights a week, twelve hour shifts.

Does your family know that you work in a bar?

No, they do not. If they knew they would think so badly of me.

Where are your kids now?

They are at home. My home here, in Phnom Penh.

Are they alone?

Yes, they are. The oldest is eleven. They are waiting for me. The elder takes care of the little one. They never fight. They know I am tired, so they are never naughty. They put themselves to bed and do not argue with me.

Do you go home with customers?

I did, but I have stopped doing so.

Why did you stop?

It is so shameful. I couldn't go on with it. I mean, thirty or forty or fifty dollars is a lot, but I just wanted to stop. I really hated it. Most of them were nice though, Western guys from here [the bar].

I see. Do you prefer working here to the factory?

Not really. But I worked for so long at the factory. But here isn't great. I want to be a cook, to open a restaurant. I love to cook.

Dai, thank you very much.

No problem. If you have any more questions, come back and ask me.

I certainly will.

This interview was conducted in Phnom Penh, 19th March 2015.

I explained my motives to the interviewee and she agreed to answer any questions I may have.

Interview conducted in Khmer.

So, hello. What is your name?

My name is So Phy. But my friends call me Phy Phy.

Ok Phy Phy. So, where are you from?

I am from Kampong Chhnang province. It is close to here, by Tonle Sap. Have you been there?

I have been through it, yes. How old are you Phy Phy?

I am twenty-two.

And do you have brothers and sisters?

Yes, I do. I am the oldest. They all live at home. I am one of five. Five children plus my mother and father. They have a shop, selling goods.

How long have you been in Phnom Penh?

Two years. I studied in Kampong Chhnang until I was eighteen, and then worked for two years at home. I helped my mother do all the cleaning and cooking. It was so boring. I wanted to come to work in Phnom Penh.

I see. Have you worked in bars these two years?

No. To start with I did cleaning. Washing clothes by hand. But that was boring too, just like at home. So I changed job, and came here, just over one year ago.

Do you like working here?

Yes, I do. I can watch TV and relax. It is much easier than cleaning all day. But the salary is poor; just $100 per month.

I see. Are you able to save money for your parents?

What do you mean?

I mean, do you save some money and send it to your parents?

No, they send money to me.

They send money to you?

Yes. $100 is not enough to live on! They sometimes send money to me, and when I visit them they give me money.

I see.

I didn't come here to earn money. I know the salary is poor. I came here to be independent, to live alone. I don't like living at home. I am twenty-two! I wanted to have my own life. See my friends, have my own money.

I see. So they know you work in a bar?

No, they don't know. I don't want them to know. They wouldn't like it. Girls who work here, people think they are bad girls, chasing money. But I work here, and I am a nice girl! I just needed a job. But I think it doesn't matter [whether they know or not]; I am the cashier. I make the drinks and calculate the bills. I don't sit with customers, I don't do that... It means I don't get many tips but I still prefer it this way, ha ha!

I see. What do you want to do after this? When you stop working in bars?

I don't know. I want to get married. But Khmer boys are no good, and I can't speak English. It will be hard for me to meet a nice foreign man. But Khmer guys always play with other girls... I don't know what I will do next!

Phy Phy, thank you

No problem!

Kampong Thom

This interview was conducted in Phnom Penh, 29th March 2015.

I explained my motives to the interviewee and she agreed to answer any questions I may have.

Interview conducted in English.

What is your name?

My name is Mao.

And where are you from Mao?

Ha ha, that is difficult to answer. I am from Kampong Thom Province. But my father is Thai, and my mother is Chinese-Vietnamese. But I was born in Cambodia and I am a Cambodian citizen.

Quite a mix! Do you have dual nationality?

No, I just have one passport. Cambodian.

I see. Can you tell me about your family?

My mother and father are dead.

Oh, Mao, I'm so sorry.

Don't worry. It has already happened. They both died. I am twenty-seven, the youngest of four. I have one sister and two brothers.

I see.

I am the manager here. Can you tell?

You seem to be in charge…

Ha ha, yes! I have been here five months. I run the whole thing. Wages, bar fines, drinks, everything. It is exhausting, but I am strong.

Very impressive.

I have no choice. My older sister is in debt. She owes people money… You know, it was this that killed my mum. My mum worried so much about the money, about the people who wanted the money, that she became sick and died. I hate my sister. But she is my sister. I have to help her. I work here at night and study during the day.

What do you study?

I study Law. I am two years in. I am doing very well! I work here at night then go to university during the day. Where in the UK are you from?

The South. Portsmouth way.

Oh, ok. I have been to Liverpool. I went for three months.

Really? Did you like it?

Yes, it was nice. I loved it, more than here. I was on holiday for three months. We travelled around, me and my boyfriend. He was a British. He was older than me, in his thirties. He broke my heart... You know, he works in the Philippines as well. I know he has a girlfriend there too, so I left him. It hurt, but I had no choice. If he wants to fuck other girls he can't fuck me.

I see.

But soon I will graduate. I am not stupid you know, and I know I am beautiful. I will do well. I know I will find a good job and a good man. And I work fucking hard. Once I graduate I will leave bars and get a really good job.

How much money do managers get?

$200 per month. But I work behind the bar. So, although I get paid more than these girls, I have to work a lot harder. I have to deal with problem customers because not all the girls can speak English. But I still get drinks and tips. So many men want to take me home and fuck me, but I am busy working. I don't need them... But sometimes I meet a nice guy. A guy I like. If he wants to take me home I get a girl to cover me and go. But most of the men are the same. I wouldn't even kiss them!

Do you like it here?

What do you think? Ha ha! I have to pay my school fees. It is hard, working by night and studying during the day, but I need to. Most of the customers here are wankers. Is that right, wankers?

You could use that word, yes.

Yes, wankers. I don't like dealing with them. But soon I will graduate. One more year!

Good for you! Does your family know you work in a bar?

I don't know. I don't care. I only cared about my mother and father. And they are dead now. I don't care what my sister and brothers think. I am earning more than they are, and they always ask me for money. They can't judge me.

Mao, thank you so much. I wish you all the best with your studies.

Thank you. I will do just fine.

Kampong Speu

This interview was conducted in Phnom Penh, 29th March 2015.

I explained my motives to the interviewee and she agreed to answer any questions I may have.

Interview conducted in English.

What is your name?

My name is Michelle

Michelle? An English name?

Yes. I like this name, it is my English name. I use it here, as most foreigners struggle with my Khmer name. But Michelle is a nice name.

Sure, I will call you Michelle. Where are you from?

Kampong Speu

And how old are you?

I am twenty-four.

Tell me about your family.

I have a mother and father, and six siblings. There are four girls and three boys. I have other family too, but they have their own houses. I don't live with them.

When did you come to Phnom Penh?

Five years ago, in 2009.

Did you come alone?

Yes, I did.

Why?

I wanted to find work.

What did you work as?

I worked in a club, on the riverside, as a waitress.

I see. What languages can you speak?

I speak Khmer, obviously, and English and Thai as well.

Can you read and write Khmer as well?

Yes, I can.

How long did you work in the club as a waitress?

For over three years. And I have been working in a bar for three weeks.

Does your family know you work in a bar?

Yes, they do.

What do they think? Have they said anything to you?

I just told them that I changed job, from working in the club to working in a bar. But I promised my mother that I will never go home with customers.

I see. What is your salary here?

$150 per month. Plus tips and 'lady drinks'.

Did you study English in school or teach yourself?

I studied at school. But I stopped. I don't want to study, I want to sleep! I want to go out and drink and have fun, not work in a classroom. And I wanted to spend time with my boyfriend.

I think that is the same for students everywhere. Are you still with that boy? Does he mind you working in a bar?

I finished with him. He wasn't a good man.

What makes you say that?

Well, he loved me, but he was very jealous. He wouldn't let me speak to other men. If he saw me speaking to another boy he would get really angry. He hit me more than once.

[Michelle demonstrates; he struck her with a closed fist]

I see. Are you looking for another boyfriend?

Later, I will find one. But not now. Right now, I don't want one. I want to find a foreign guy, they are much nicer. I want to leave Cambodia, live somewhere else. I'm finished with Khmer men, they're no good.

When you stop working here, what do you want to do?

I don't know yet. Maybe I will let you know another day.

Great, thank you very much.

No problem. Speak later

This interview was conducted in Phnom Penh, 29th March 2015.

I explained my motives to the interviewee and she agreed to answer any questions I may have.

Interview conducted in English and Khmer.

So, what is your name?

My name is Srey Ya.

And where are you from?

I am from Kampong Speu province.

And how old are you?

Ha ha, older than you! I am thirty-one. You are my little brother!

That's fine big sister! How long have you been in bars?

Umm… Well, I was here for a few years and then I met a man. So I left.

Oh, I see. Did he take you out of work?

No, but I lived with him. So it meant I didn't have to pay for rent, and it meant that I could do what I wanted to do.

What did you do?

I sold food! I have always wanted to make my own food and sell it. Do you know those fried vegetable cakes?

Severed with chili sauce?

Yes. I sold those, and mango salad. The money wasn't very good but I really enjoyed it. I didn't have to work nights, and I got to cook nice food. I was so happy.

So why are you back here?

I broke up with him. I moved out.

What happened?

He turned gay

Sorry?

He is gay now. He always used to have time to go to Thailand to play with boys. But we stopped having sex. We did to start with, and then he started seeing boys and then we broke up. I was with him for about five months.

I see.

It was hard. I love him you know, I love him. How can he do this to me? When he broke up with me I was so sad. I asked 'Why are you doing this? I love you! I love you' but he just kept saying it had changed. We stopped having sex and he would only see boys. So I moved out and I am back here.

You couldn't continue selling food?

The money wasn't as good. I had to buy the ingredients. And I have two girls from my old husband that I have to support. I get a salary here, plus tips. But when I sold food if I didn't sell much I didn't get much money. No salary.

Can you tell me about him? Your ex-husband?

He was a Khmer. We met about ten years ago and I have two children with him. My two girls.

[Srey Ya scrolls through her phone and shows me a picture of two young girls smiling at the camera, standing in the doorway of a traditional wooden house]

Aren't they lovely? Neang is seven and Pich is eight. I love them so much. They are at my home in Kampong Speu. They live with my parents. I wouldn't like that have them here. Phnom Penh is so busy and the air is unclean. I can't see them often, I miss them very much.

Do any of your family know you work in a bar?

No. I don't tell them. But I think they might know. There are pictures on my Facebook of me dressed like this [Srey Ya is wearing a short, low cut dress with heavy make-up] but I have never actually said. But I told them all when I was selling food. I used to send photos of my food, for them to see.

Yeah, I see

I mean, they know I had a foreign boyfriend. They saw the pictures. And I did not lie about him. Maybe they have worked out that I work in a bar. But it isn't like I sleep with customers. I had a boyfriend and I was a good girlfriend to him. I still miss him. I still love him. But he is gay. I cannot change him.

So what do you want to do when you finish here?

Sell food again! You know, it is hard. I want to go back to Kampong Speu, to be with my children. But selling food in the provinces is very bad money. If I want to sell food I have to be away from my daughters. It is very hard. But they live with my parents who are very good people. I just miss them.

Srey Ya, thank you for talking to me. It must have been hard to talk about.

It is ok. It doesn't matter. It is just my life. Speak to you another time.

Kampong Som

This interview was conducted in Kampong Som, 28th March 2015.

I explained my motives to the interviewee and she agreed to answer any questions I may have.

Interview conducted in Khmer.

Ok then, so, what is your name?

My name is Boah

Can you tell me a bit about yourself? Where you are from, your family?

Well, my name is Boah and I am twenty-two. Um, I can speak a little bit of English, but only speak. And I am from Kampong Som...

You are from here?

Yes, correct. I am one of eight, and we all live together with our parents.

Eight! Wow, mealtimes must be crazy!

Ha ha, yes! Five boys and three girls, including me.

Do they work too?

Yes, they do. Well, the boys do. And I work here. But my sisters both have foreign boyfriends who send them money, so they don't have to work.

Where are their boyfriends from?

One is from England, and the other, I think, is from Australia. Sorry, I have forgotten.

So you're the only girl that works. Do your parents know you work in a bar?

[Boah nods]

Do they mind?

No, they don't mind. I'm a cashier, they know I don't dress like those other girls [Boah gestures toward the other girls in the bar wearing revealing clothes] or have to sit with customers. I just get to sit here and take the money.

Do you like it here? Working in a bar?

Half-half. When it is quiet I don't get any tips. But when it is busy I end up getting drunk and having a hangover! It is hard! But it is better than my old job.

Yes, I understand. What was your old job?

Factory work. The salary is the same as here, but that work is exhausting. You have to concentrate, and the boss was always watching us. Like a policeman! Not fun.

So what is your salary then?

$120 per month. But here I get lady drinks and tips too! I will open a shop after this. I will save my money and me and my brothers and sisters can save together and buy a shop. Open a shop.

A shop? And sell what?

Things. Shirts and shoes, things, everything!

Did you go to school?

Yes, we all did. But it gets more expensive as you get older. And when you are studying you cannot work and earn money. So I left. I left when I was eighteen. Then I worked as a cleaner, and now I work here.

Boah, thank you so much for talking to me.

No worries. See you later!

Kandal

This interview was conducted in Phnom Penh, 17th March 2015.

I explained my motives to the interviewee and she agreed to answer any questions I may have.

Interview conducted in Khmer and English.

So, what is your name?

My name is Di.

Where are you from?

I am from Kandal province

How old are you?

I am 30 years old.

When did you move to Phnom Penh?

I moved here seventeen years ago. I came with a friend.

Did you study?

No, I worked. I worked for an NGO which helps young children, mainly girls. I made cakes.

How long did you work there for?

Ten years

Why did you leave that job?

The money wasn't very good. Just $90 per month. But now my friend is on $300 a month working there.

And when did you start working in bars?

When I left the NGO. A friend got me a job in this bar; her, there [Di gestures to another girl].

Do you speak any languages?

Just Khmer and a little bit of English. I learnt at the NGO. I used to be able to read and write English too, but I have since forgotten. I can still speak a little bit though.

I see. Have you ever been abroad or anything like that?

Just to Vietnam.

Where is your family now?

They are still in Kandal province. I am one of six; three boys and three girls. My parents have died. My father died twenty years ago, my mother about seven years ago. My little sister has also died.

How did they die?

They all died of illnesses. My little sister died so suddenly. She fell sick and within five days died. I never knew it was so serious. I always told her dying people don't eat, so as long as she continued eating she wouldn't die. She passed away a few days later. When she died I changed. She used to always ask me to go out dancing, and I always said no. But after she died I changed. Now I love to drink and go dancing and have fun. Everyone says that I have changed, but I just think I am happy.

My condolences...

It is ok.

Where do you live now?

In Steung Mean Chey, in Phnom Penh. Quite far from here.

[The interview is paused whilst Di and another girl converse; it seems they live very close-by one another and have been paying for separate *tuk-tuks* for some time]

Do you live alone?

No, with my older sister.

What does she do?

She works in a factory, making clothes.

Does she know you work in a bar?

No, she does not. She would disapprove. She is on $200 per month.

What about you?

Ha ha, a lot!

How so?

I go home with customers.

I see.

And at $50 a time, I can make money! Sometimes one per night, sometimes more. I can earn a lot… I have forgotten how many men I have been with. It isn't important. Maybe it was before, but now it is not important. It is my life and I am earning lots of money.

When did you start sleeping with customers?

Seven years ago, when I first started.

Your first time was with a customer?

No, just a stranger. He asked me to go home with him, and I went. Not a boyfriend, not a customer. I did not know him.

Are you safe when you do this? Do you go to the doctor?

Yes, I am not stupid. I always use a condom. I get checked regularly at the local clinic run by an NGO. I try to get the other girls to go too.

Do you have any children of your own?

No, I do not.

Do you want to have a family?

Ha ha, no, because I can't have fun! Maybe when I am forty, but not now.

What do you want to do after you finish working here?

I want to sell food, snacks, with my sister at our house in Phnom Penh. I want to sell cakes again!

Di, thank you very much

Not at all. It has been fun!

This interview was conducted in Phnom Penh, 20th March 2015.

I explained my motives to the interviewee and she agreed to answer any questions I may have.

Interview conducted in Khmer and English.

What is your name?

Moch.

Where are you from Moch?

Kandal Province. It is very beautiful, have you been there?

I have only been through it. Can you tell me about your family?

They live in Kandal. I have two brothers and one sister, and they all still live in Kandal. They are all married. My father died a few years ago, he was sick for a long time. We couldn't afford treatment, medicine, so he died. It was very hard for us.

I see. I am sorry.

It is ok. I don't have any children. I used to have a Khmer boyfriend, but he was bad. He was like a butterfly.

Sorry?

Like a butterfly. He had many girls, always going after different girls. I left him and came to Phnom Penh.

So you came alone? How long have you been here?

Yes, I came alone. I have been in Phnom Penh for three years now.

Have you always worked in bars?

No, I have only worked here for three months. I used to work in a house.

A house?

Yes, in a house. I made clothes, dresses.

Oh, a factory?

Yes, but it was in a house. I made clothes. But I hated that work. It was exhausting! And the salary was poor, just $100. Not enough to live on.

And here? What is the salary here?

The same, $100. But here I get tips and lady drinks. Every lady drink I get I am given 6000 riels. Also, if I go with customers, I can get extra money…

I see. Did you go to school when you were younger?

Ha ha, not really. I would go for a few months, and then have to stop. When my parents ran out of money me and my siblings had to stop going to school. We used to help my mother sell fish in the market. I was happy, I used to spend time with my family. But it means that I never learnt English. And I can only read and write a little bit [of Khmer].

What do you want to do when you leave here?

I don't know. I want a family. I am thirty, I need to have a baby soon. I think that is most important.

Moch, thank you very much.

This interview was conducted in Phnom Penh, 5th April 2015.

I explained my motives to the interviewee and she agreed to answer any questions I may have.

Interview conducted in Khmer.

What is your name?

My name is Piah.

Where are you from?

I am from Kandal province.

And how old are you?

I am thirty-five.

When did you come to Phnom Penh?

I came in 1989.

Was that for work?

No, for studying. I came to go to school. The schools in Phnom Penh are better than in Kandal.

Did you come alone?

No, I came with my family. They still live in Phnom Penh, but my mother has since died. She was sick, she had cancer. The doctor is too expensive, we couldn't afford to have her treated.

My condolences.

It is ok, thank you

What did you do after you finished studying? Did you work?

Yes, I worked in a market.

What did you sell?

I sold everything. Fish, food, things.

And how long have you worked in a bar for?

I have worked here for three months.

Do you have a boyfriend?

Yes, I do. He is from Australia. He lives there, but comes to visit.

I see. Do you go home with customers?

Sometimes, not every time.

Why do you go home with customers?

Because my boyfriend doesn't give me enough money. I must provide for my family. I am one of eight; I have four brothers and three sisters. Well, three brothers now; one of them died. He was knocked off his motorbike. You must be careful on the roads here... He gives me enough money for me, for me to live on, but I have to send some to my brothers and sisters. If I go home with customers then we can all live better,

I see. What languages can you speak, Piah?

Khmer, obviously, and a little bit of English.

Does your mother and your siblings know you work in a bar?

No, they don't know!

What do you think they would feel about you working here?

They would think badly of me, that I am immoral. Girls who work here aren't good girls, and they would think I am like them.

So you didn't tell them?

No, I lied. I told them I work in a factory, not a bar.

I see. What is your salary here?

$100

And you get to keep tips, yes?

Yes, but it isn't very much.

When you stop working here, what do you want to do?

I want to work in a restaurant, to cook. I want to open my own restaurant; I love to cook, I am a really good cook!

Do you have any children?

Yes, two. I used to be married to a Cambodian man. He has remarried since. I was only eighteen at the time, and he was thirty-eight. I had two daughters with him.

What happened?

I went to work, but he didn't. He was lazy; I had to do everything, whilst he did nothing. He used to hit me as well.

I see...

Now I have a boyfriend I want to stop having sex. But before I met him I used to a lot, I had to. He loves me, and wants me to stop having sex. But he doesn't know when he will return. But I needed the money, you know? $50 is a lot of money, and my family need it. Now I can go less, now I have a boyfriend.

Piah, thank you very much for telling me this. I know it must be very difficult for you to relive these details.

No worries. It is good to know you care. See you when you come back!

So, what is your name?

My name is Somaly.

How old are you?

I am twenty-five years old.

Where are you from?

I am from Kandal, but I have lived in Phnom Penh since 2009.

I see. Tell me about your family.

I am one of two; I have a younger sister, who is eighteen. She is studying in Kampong Som. She will leave high school soon. My mother and father live in Kandal.

So you came to Phnom Penh alone?

Yes, on my own.

Does your family know you worked in a bar?

No, they don't. I would never let them know.

What did you do when you first came here?

I studied English, in a church. Then I studied at Norton University. Economic Banking and Finance.

Do you have a boyfriend?

Yes, I do, but he doesn't know I used to work in a bar. If he knew he would be so angry with me!

Where did you meet him? In the bar?

No, at university. He is a Khmer. He is lovely, I love him so much. He is such a nice man. He cares so much for me.

How long did you work in a bar for?

Five months. But I have stopped now. I don't want to work in a bar; I want to work in a bank.

Why did you start working in a bar?

Now I have finished my studies I want to work in a bank. But I needed money to cover my school fees. I have finished studying, so I have stopped at the bar.

What was your salary in the bar?

$120 per month. But I got tips and lady drinks as well. Usually an additional $100 per month.

Did you go home with customers?

Yes, a few times… five times, if I remember right. I didn't like it, but I needed the money. As simple as that. Sometimes I got $50, sometimes $70, sometimes $100.

Were you safe?

Yes, I never forgot to use protection.

Where were these men from?

Australia, US, Britain. I'm not sure, but they were English speakers.

Did you lose your virginity to a customer?

No, to my boyfriend.

Sorry, to a previous boyfriend?

No, this boyfriend, the one I have now.

Oh, so you broke up with him and slept with those men, and have gotten back with him since then?

No, I have always been with him, even when I went home with those men. That's why I don't want him to know. I have been with him seven years, and we are very happy together. I wouldn't jeopardise our relationship…

That is fine, we don't need to discuss it further. Actually, I think I'm about done. Do you have anything to add?

No, not really. Listen, don't think badly of me. My boyfriend used to give me money, but it wasn't enough. I had no choice. I didn't want to beg for more money from him. I didn't want to do it, I didn't want to go home with them. But I have graduated now, now I can get a good job and have a good life.

Ok, thank you very much for telling me this. I do understand, life is hard here. I am glad everything has worked out.

Thanks!

This interview was conducted in Phnom Penh, 17th March 2015.

I explained my motives to the interviewee and she agreed to answer any questions I may have.

Interview conducted in English.

So, what is your name?

Srey Nut.

And where are you from?

Kandal province.

Yes, ok. So, how old are you?

Ha ha, I am old. Twenty-eight! Twenty-eight and unmarried, ha ha!

When did you come to Phnom Penh?

I came here nearly ten years ago. I came here on my own; there are no jobs in Kandal province. And for girls it is really hard. Men can get into business or whatever, but not girls. So I came here.

Have you always worked in bars here?

Yes, I have. So I came when I was eighteen, and I have worked in various bars… I want to find a foreign guy, a nice foreign guy.

I see

I have had many boyfriends here, from bars. Before you ask, yes, I go home with customers. It is so easy. And if I get on with the guy, if he likes me and wants to give me money, then I can be his girlfriend. I have a child from one of them.

With a foreign guy?

Yeah. A British. He is so fat now, he is 200 kilograms. But he used to be slim. I have a child with him. Wait a moment…

[Srey Nut perused through her phone, and conjured up a picture of a mixed-race boy about four years old]

Cute huh? He is at my home, in Kandal. He doesn't live in Phnom Penh. I work too much, he wouldn't like it here.

So you were married to this British guy?

No, I'm just his girlfriend. I was with him for one year. Then I found another guy, an Australian. He worked here, but he was a bad guy. He always used to play in other bars, play with other girls. You know, he was playing in another bar with some girl. And one of my friends saw her, saw him. So I called him and asked 'Hey, where are you?' and he said 'Oh, I'm in Kampot, I'm in Kampot. I'm on business.' He's a fucking liar. So I went to the bar and slapped him and called him a motherfucker. That was it, finished.

So you're single now?

No, I have a new boyfriend from New Zealand. He is really nice, but young. Just twenty-five, younger than me. So he has no money. He is working in New Zealand, and will save his money and come back here to live with me.

I see. So, does your family know you work in a bar?

Ha ha ha, of course! Of course they know, I have a mixed-blood baby! They know I had a foreign boyfriend. You know, they were really annoyed. I was not married and yet I was pregnant with a foreigner. But they love me and my boy is beautiful. They love him too. He stays there.

Do you have a plan for after you stop working in bars?

Well, when my boyfriend comes back I can live with him. I won't need to work. I can spend time with him and my son.

Kratie

This interview was conducted in Phnom Penh, 17th February 2015.

I explained my motives to the interviewee and she agreed to answer any questions I may have.

Interview conducted in Khmer and English.

So, what is your name?

My name is Chean.

And where are you from?

I am from Kratie.

Kratie? I like it there. I have been there before. How old are you Chean?

I am thirty-two years old.

When did you come to Phnom Penh? Why did you come?

I came in 2000, when I was seventeen. I worked in a factory making clothes. The materials came from China, and the finished goods were sent to the UK.

When did you stop working in the factory?

2010.

Why did you stop working there?

The salary wasn't good enough, just $90 a month. It is not enough to live on.

What were the hours like?

Ten hours a day, six days a week.

How many are there in your family?

I have one older sister and two older brothers.

Are you married?

I was married between 2003 and 2008.

Why did you divorce?

He was unfaithful. I am on a lower social level than him. His family didn't like me.

So you live alone now?

No, I have a child. She is two years and eight months old.

So not from your previous marriage?

No. From a [different] previous relationship.

So how long have you been working in bars?

I started in 2010. I left to have my child, and started again.

Why did you decide to work in a bar?

I need the money. I can't write Khmer or English, I only spent three years in school. I can't find a good job, just here or the factory. I need as much money as I can get to support my child.

How much is your salary?

Here? $90 per month.

So it is the same as the factory?

Yes, but here I get tips. And when you buy a Lady Drink I get 5000 riels ($1.25).

I see

And here I have the opportunity to meet a man. That is what I want, that is what all these girls want. Meeting a Western man is a way to stop being poor.

Does your family know you work here? Do you parents know?

My father has passed away.

My apologies.

It is alright. He had an illness. But my mother does not know I work here. She would be very angry if she knew. I send money to her each month, as much as I can. If she knew where the money came from she would be very angry, and would be ashamed of me.

Do you like working here? Do you like the work?

No, I don't like working here. I feel angry with myself. When I have a boyfriend I will stop. I want to find a boyfriend here. I have a boyfriend now, but it is not a proper relationship; he is married. It makes me sad to know. He knows I work here, I met him here. He sends me money every month, but it isn't much. Not enough to stop working. He is American. If he comes back I will live with him and love him and I can stop working here.

Chean, thank you very much.

Not at all.

Phnom Penh

This interview was conducted in Phnom Penh, 5th April 2015.

I explained my motives to the interviewee and she agreed to answer any questions I may have.

Interview conducted in Khmer.

What is your name?

My name is Chen Da

How old are you?

I am twenty-five.

Where are you from?

I am from Phnom Penh.

You still live with your family?

Yes, with my family. My mum and dad and my siblings.

How many of you are there?

Five, including me. All girls! I am number four, so three are older than me and one younger.

Do they work?

They work in a factory, making clothes. They have a better salary than me, but I am lazy. Working here is much easier. Have you ever seen inside a factory? I mean here, in Cambodia? So tiring, and really hot. Here I can sit and relax. We have Wi-Fi!

I see. What languages can you speak?

Just Khmer. I can't read and write very much though…

How long have you worked in bars?

Just one month. I am new to all of this.

Why did you decide to work in a bar?

I don't know, I just wanted to.

What made you want to work in a bar?

I don't have any money. A job is a job.

What did you do before working here?

I studied. I have stopped already. I studied Khmer and English.

Do your parents know you work in a bar?

Yes, they know

What do they think about it?

They don't mind. They respect my decision.

Do you have a boyfriend?

No, I don't. I'm all alone, ha ha! I want a nice foreign boy. Foreign men are nicer than Khmer men. It is easy to meet foreigners here [in bars].

Do you go with customers?

No, I don't. I am a virgin. I want to find a nice husband, not just go for sex. Do you understand what I mean?

Yes, I do. Do you like working here?

No, not really. I want to stop.

I see... But earlier you said that you wanted to work here, that it is better than the factory.

Well, sometimes it is good, sometimes bad. I don't really know what I want.

What is your salary?

$100 per month. Plus about $50 in tips and lady drinks.

When you stop working here, what do you want to do?

I want to study again. Study English. [She paused] I don't want to leave Cambodia. I am Khmer. But foreign boys are so much better. Khmer boys don't respect their wives, they are abusive. That is what I have heard. You see it often, here, in bars. Women who have had to leave their husbands. I don't want that. I know lots of women who work here who already have kids, who have gotten divorced. They want a foreign husband too.

I have come across it, yes. I think we are about done, thank you very much.

No worries. See you soon!

*This interview was conducted in Phnom Penh,
15th April 2015.*

*I explained my motives to the interviewee and she
agreed to answer any questions I may have.*

Interview conducted in Khmer.

What is your name?

My name is Nida. You can call me Oun Nida if you
like.

Sure. So, how old are you?

I am twenty-three

*Yes, you are younger than me. I will call you Oun. So, Oun,
where are you from?*

I am from Phnom Penh. You know the river here?

Of course.

I live on the other side, near the Sokha Hotel.

Yes, I know it.

I live there.

Do you live alone? Or with your family?

I live with my family. Mother and father and my
siblings.

99

I see. How long have you worked here then, in a bar?

Just three weeks. It is very different to what I used to do…

What did you do before this then?

I used to work in a factory. A small factory near my home making curtains.

So why have you changed work, and come here?

It is horrible work [in a factory]. So exhausting. Many girls work in bars, so I thought I would try it.

And the salary? Is it better here?

I don't know. I was on $120 in the factory. But I have just been here for three weeks, I don't know what the salary is here.

I see. But you get tips and lady drinks?

I don't know. I haven't had any yet, ha ha! I am shy, and can't speak English. I am shy speaking with foreigners.

Can you speak any other languages?

No, not really. I studied English at school but not much. I cannot speak it. The teacher wasn't very good you see.

I see. So, when you stop working here, what do you want to do?

I don't know yet. I am old… Twenty three is old for a Khmer girl.

What do you mean?

I need to get married really. I know my parents want me to get married, but I don't know any nice boys. I don't want my parents to find a boy for me.

I understand. Do they know you work here?

Yes, they do. I mean I used to work days and now I work nights.

Do they mind?

Yes, they don't like it. But they know I hated it in the factory. Maybe I can find a nice boy here, but I can't speak English. Only foreigners come here.

Oun, thank you very much. It has been very interesting for me.

No problem. I think what you are doing is good. I think that many girls here have little choice. People need to understand that.

This interview was conducted in Phnom Penh, 15th April 2015.

I explained my motives to the interviewee and she agreed to answer any questions I may have.

Interview conducted in Khmer.

So, what is your name?

Srey Pich

And where are you from?

Here. From Phnom Penh. I live near the Royal Palace.

Oh right. Do you live with your family?

Yes. My father and my step-mother and my brothers and sisters.

And how long have you worked in bars?

I don't work here.

Sorry, I don't understand.

I mean, I come and play here but I don't have a salary. I don't have to come.

You don't get a salary?

Correct. I just get lady drinks and tips. Every lady drink I get I am given $1.5. But I don't get many. I am twenty-five. Some customers like old ladies, and I am too young for them. But some customers like younger girls, just eighteen or nineteen, and I am too old for them.

I see. Why don't you work full time and get a salary too?

It would interfere with my sleep. And I study English. Every day, one hour. Seven dollars a week. So expensive! I am working on my conversation. I can also speak some Japanese!

Very impressive.

Yes. If you can speak Japanese or English or Korean you can get a good job. So my studies are very important. Anyway, I don't like staying at home. I hate my step-mother. You see these scars? Here?

[Srey Pich turns her head from side to side, pointing to several scars on her cheeks and chin. They look similar to the scars left after severe acne.]

My step-mother did this. She hit me when she was cooking. She used a hot spatula. It was very hot and she hit my face with it. I hate her. So I prefer to come here and earn some money and relax.

So you like working here?

Hmm. Sometimes. It is better than working in a factory, or cleaning. And I can speak English with some customers, practise.

Yes. So what do you want to do after you finish your studies?

I don't know yet. Once I can speak English I will be able to find a good job. I don't know what I will do yet, but I think once I can speak English I will be able to get a good job so I can buy my own house.

Srey Pich, thank you very much

No problem, thank you!

This interview was conducted in Phnom Penh, 16th March 2015.

I explained my motives to the interviewee and she agreed to answer any questions I may have.

Interview conducted in Khmer.

So, what is your name?

My name is Srey Nida. Just call me Nida, that is fine.

How old are you Nida?

I am twenty-four. But it is my birthday next week! I am very excited. I will meet my friends and go for a meal and have a cake!

Happy birthday then! And how long have you worked in bars?

I have only worked in this bar. I have been here four months. I used to study English, for seven years. From when I was seventeen to this year. But I cannot speak it very well. I think my teacher was not very good. Or maybe I am stupid. I don't know. Once I finished my studies I came here.

I see. And where are you from?

I am from here, Phnom Penh. I live with my family not far from here. I live with my mother and father and siblings.

Do they know you work in a bar?

Yes, they know. I told them, I didn't want to lie to them. But I don't think it matters. I don't go home with customers. Some of the girls here do. The massge customers and touch them and kiss them, and then take them to a hotel. I could never do that. I am too shy. I am a virgin, I could not do these things. I just sit and talk, like now. Actually, I did lie to them…

About what?

I told them I'm a cashier. I told them I do the money and drinks. They don't know I sit with customers. If they knew that some customers try and touch me they would be so ashamed of me.

I understand. What is the salary like here?

I get $100 per month, plus tips and lady drinks. But because I don't touch the customers they don't speak with me very much. If I massage them they would buy me more, but I cannot do it.

Do you like working here?

Um, yes. I have never worked another job before. This is my first job after my studies. But I know some girls who work here who used to work in factories making clothes. They said that work is horrible. Here we can sit and relax. We have wi-fi and I can have cold water. And customers buy me coca cola or Malibu. This job is good.

Ok. And what do you wish to do when you stop working here?

I want to open a salon. Look…

[Srey Nida gestures to her cheeks and eyes, which have been made up impeccably, and to her nails which are strong and beautifully painted]

I did these myself. If you go to the market it would cost you $2 for the nails and $2 for the make-up, but I do it myself and I do it better. If I open a salon I can do it every day and I can earn more. I already have lots of paint and make up. But I need the money to rent a shop and things.

That sounds like a great plan. Nida, thank you very much.

No problem. Thank you for talking with me. It has been fun.

Prey Veng

This interview was conducted in Phnom Penh, 16th March 2015.

I explained my motives to the interviewee and she agreed to answer any questions I may have.

Interview conducted in Khmer.

What is your name?

My name is Chor Vi

How old are you?

I am nineteen years old.

Where are you from?

I am from Prey Veng Province

Did you come to Phnom Penh alone?

No, I came with my parents and some of my siblings.

Do you still live with them?

No, I live here [above the bar].

How many brothers and sister do you have?

Yes, I am one of six.

Wow, big family! How many are boys, and how many are girls?

Two boys, four girls.

Did they come with you to Phnom Penh?

Most of them did, but one of my sisters stayed in Prey Veng.

Do they work?

Yes, they work in a factory making clothes.

Where do they live? With your parents?

Yes, in Steung Mean Chey, in Phnom Penh. It is quite far from here.

Did you attend school?

Yes, I studied for seven years.

Did you study English?

No, I did not.

What languages can you speak?

Just Khmer.

But you can read and write, as well as speak, Khmer?

Yes.

[At this, Chor Vi took up my pocket dictionary and proceeded to read some of the words out to me]

Do your parents know you work in a bar?

Yes, they do.

What do they think? Did they say anything to you?

They don't mind, I think they understand. But my older brothers mind, they really hate it.

What did they say?

They just said that they didn't want me to work in a bar, that I should find a better job. But it isn't as simple as that.

How long have you worked here?

I have only worked here for five days.

Do you like working here?

Yes, I do.

Why?

The work is easy. I don't get exhausted working here. I can just sit and relax, chat with the girls and speak with customers. And customers buy me drinks! They buy me cola and beer, ha ha!

What did you do for work before coming here?

I worked in a factory making clothes. It was very tiring, and very hot. I really didn't like it.

How much did you earn per month working in the factory?

$130

And here? How much do you earn per month here?

$70

So, you get paid less working here than you did working in the factory. Why did you change job?

I wanted to leave home, to get away. My father beats my mother. I hated having to see it. I wanted to leave so I wouldn't have to witness it. Now I live here.

Why does he do that?

I don't know. He doesn't drink, he isn't drunk. But my mother drinks now...

I see. It must be difficult.

Yes, it is. I don't know why he does it. He never used to. I think he has just stopped loving her. I hated seeing it, I had to get out.

Do you go home with customers?

No, I don't.

Why not?

I have never been with a man before. I don't have a boyfriend, and I don't want one...

Too young?

[Chor laughs]

Yes!

What do you want to do after this? After you stop working here?

When I have a husband I will study English. If he can support me enough so I can stop working, I will study full time. If you speak English, and read and write, you can get a good job.

Chor, thank you so much.

Wait, I have to say something else.

Yes, what?

[Chor leaned in closer and lowered her voice]

I do have a boyfriend. I lied.

Oh, I see. Why did you lie?

Because I don't want the girls here to know. Maybe they will think badly of me, if I have a boyfriend and yet I work here. They might think badly of me when I speak with customers.

I see. I don't think they'd care. Some of these girls have boyfriends as well. Does he know you work here?

No, he doesn't. He works very hard, and always tries to give me money, but it is never very much. Now I have moved out I have to work. He would feel so bad if he knew he couldn't support me properly.

Thank you for telling me this. I won't tell any of the girls, not to worry.

Ok, thanks.

This interview was conducted in Phnom Penh, 5th April 2015.

I explained my motives to the interviewee and she agreed to answer any questions I may have.

Interview conducted in Khmer.

What is your name?

My name is Chentou.

How old are you?

I am eighteen years old.

And where are you from? Which province?

Prey Veng Province

Tell me about your family.

I have two little sisters, a mum and dad. My parents are farmers. They are all still in Prey Veng. My parents grow rice, and my sisters help them. We also have some buffalo.

When did you come to Phnom Penh?

I came three years ago. I came to study. The schools in Prey Veng aren't any good.

Did you come alone?

Yes, I did.

And now you have finished your studies?

Yes, I have.

What languages can you speak?

Khmer and a little bit of English. I studied English for a short while. I can read and write Khmer too!

How long have you worked in bars?

I have only worked in one, and for just one month.

How much do you get per month?

Um, $100

Do you get tips?

Yes, but I don't know how much yet. I haven't had my salary yet.

Do you live alone?

No, I live with three other girls. They work in bars too.

Do you go home with customers?

No, I don't. I don't want to.

Do you parents know you work in a bar?

[Chentou paused]

Yes, they know.

What do they think? Have they said anything to you?

They don't like it. But I told them I don't go home with customers, and they believe me. I don't like it here, but I have to provide for my family. I have two little sisters, and they need to study. It is important they study. I will send them $50 when I get paid.

Do you have a boyfriend?

No, I don't want one, not yet.

When you stop working here, what do you want to do?

I want to study again, study English. I want to go to America!

I think that is everything I wanted to ask. Thank you so much

No worries. I understand why you are doing this, I think it is good. Best of luck

Thanks

This interview was conducted in Phnom Penh, 9th July 2015.

I explained my motives to the interviewee and she agreed to answer any questions I may have.

Interview conducted in Khmer.

So, what is your name?

My name is Panha.

How old are you Panha?

I am nineteen years old.

And where are you from?

I am from Prey Veng Province.

Tell me about your family.

Well, I have a father, but my mother died in 2008. I have one brother and one sister.

I am sorry to hear about your mother. How did she die?

She was ill. The doctor didn't know what was wrong with her, but it was something inside her stomach. We didn't have the money to go to the hospital for an operation. She died back in 2008.

I really am sorry to hear that. Thank you for telling me. Did you come to Phnom Penh alone?

No, I came with my brother and sister.

Do you still live with them?

Yes, I still live with them; the three of us together.

And your dad is still in Prey Veng? When did you come to Phnom Penh?

Yes, he is still there [in Prey Veng]. I came here two years ago.

So, you came to Phnom Penh in 2013. What did you do when you first arrived?

I worked on my studies.

And what did you study?

I studied English.

I see. How many languages can you speak?

Just two. A little bit of English and Khmer.

Great. Ok, now about the bar. How long have you worked here? Do you like it?

Four months. No, I don't like it, but I need the money. I have to work.

Why don't you like it? Why not move to another job, at the market or factory or shop?

During the day I am busy studying English. I don't have time to relax! Then every night I have to come and work in the bar. It means I can earn money at night, and study during the day.

I see. Does your family know you live here? I mean, your brother and sister know you work nights…

My sister knows. I had to tell someone. She helps me wash my clothes. If my brother saw the clothes I wear here he would know I work in a bar or club. He just thinks I work nights in a factory. That is common. My father thinks the same. I don't want them to know. They would feel ashamed, and feel that they haven't supported me enough.

I understand entirely. What do you want to do when you stop working here?

I don't know yet. Go back to Prey Veng. It is a poor province, but very beautiful. My father is there, and so are my aunts and uncles and my cousins. If I could save up my wages I could go back, maybe open a shop at the market. I want to cook. After my mother died I and my sister cooked for the family. Really delicious Khmer food. I could sell it.

Thank you very much for speaking with me

Not a problem. I like to meet new people.

This interview was conducted in Phnom Penh, 31st March 2015.

I explained my motives to the interviewee and she agreed to answer any questions I may have.

Interview conducted in Khmer.

What is your name?

My name is Srey Puon

Where are you from?

I am from Prey Veng province.

And how old are you?

I am thirty years old.

Could you tell me about your family?

I don't have a father. My mother is still alive, and she is still in Prey Veng. I am one of four children; there are three girls and one boy.

Could you tell me about what happened to your father?

He died from stomach troubles, intestinal complications. He didn't smoke or drink or anything like that. He went to the doctor, who tried to help, but they couldn't save him. He died in 2000, 15 years ago.

My condolences. What languages can you speak?

Just Khmer.

But you can read and write it?

Yes

When did you come to Phnom Penh?

I came in 2009, six years ago.

Did you come alone?

Yes, I did. My siblings stayed in Prey Veng.

What about now? Are they still in Prey Veng?

No, they are here now, in Phnom Penh. My brother does welding in a workshop, and my sisters work in bars, similar to this one. Quite close to here actually.

Why did you come to Phnom Penh in 2009?

I needed to find work. My mother doesn't have any money. My siblings help her, and send her money too, but at the time [in 2009] they had very little for her. I decided to come and find better work in the city.

How long have you worked in bars?

Two years.

When you first came to Phnom Penh what did you work as?

I was a cleaner. I worked in someone's house. I had to do everything, you know? Like wash the dishes, wash the clothes, mop the floors, everything.

How much did they pay you?

Just $30 per month. But I lived there, and they provided me food. I didn't have to buy my own food or pay for rent.

I see.

So I could live, I could eat and live, but I could never save money for my parents. I couldn't buy anything more than a few new tops each month, or go for a coffee.

You prefer it here?

Yes, I do. It is much easier. Although I have to pay rent, I have my own money. And I can save up. I can save all my tips and take them home.

Yes. What do you want to do in the future?

Have a family. If I can save up I can have a family. But I need to find a nice man first. I want children. I am thirty, and that is old in Cambodia. Then I can have a family and look after my babies. That is what I want.

Srey Puon, thank you very much.

No problem. I have enjoyed speaking with you.

Siem Reap

This interview was conducted in Kampong Som, 27th March 2015.

I explained my motives to the interviewee and she agreed to answer any questions I may have.

Interview conducted in Khmer.

Ok, so, what is your name?

My name is Srey Bai.

And where are you from Srey Bai?

I am from Siem Reap. It is a very famous province! Have you been?

Yes, I have. It is very impressive.

Yes, I am glad you like it there.

How old are you?

I am twenty-three.

Please tell me about your family.

Well, I have a mother and father, and I am one of six; I have one sister, and four brothers.

And did you go to school? Did you ever study English?

Yes, I went to school. I can read and write Khmer very well! I can also speak some Thai, and a little bit of English. My school was not very good though, and my English is quite poor.

I see. When did you come to Kampong Som? And did you come alone?

Um, I came when I was seventeen, so in 2009... yes, 2009. I came with my siblings, and we lived together.

What did you do? Did you work?

No, I studied. I studied for one year, but then I ran out of money. I had to terminate my studies early, and started work in a restaurant.

I see. So, how long have you worked in bars?

I have worked here for two months.

Why did you choose to work here? Why did you leave the restaurant?

I wanted to learn English, and many of the customers here are English speaking, you know? Australians, British, Americans. I can speak English here, and improve.

But, surely foreigners eat at the restaurant too? The restaurants here have many foreigners.

No, I didn't work close to here. I worked in a Khmer restaurant. Foreigners rarely ate there, it was mainly Khmer people.

Oh, I see. But do you still live with your siblings?

No, I moved out. None of my family know I work in a bar. They would hate to know that I worked here. I cannot tell them.

Didn't your siblings ask questions when you moved out?

No, I just said that I have another job and moved out. I live alone now, close to here.

Ok, I understand. What do you think about working here? Do you like it?

Yes, the work is easy. I can sit down and eat and talk with my friends, whilst in the restaurant I had to carry heavy plates and do lots of washing up. But I haven't learnt much English. All the customers speak so fast, I cannot understand them. And there is loud music… but the work is much better.

Do you go home with customers?

No, I don't. I have my salary, which is enough. I chose to work here to learn English, not go home with men.

I see. And what do you wish to do after you finish working here?

I want to go back to Siem Reap. I want to go back and live with my parents there. I will find a job there, I'm not fussy.

Ok, thank you Srey Bai, I think that is everything.

No problem. Speak again soon!

Svay Rieng

This interview was conducted in Phnom Penh, 28th March 2015.

I explained my motives to the interviewee and she agreed to answer any questions I may have.

Interview conducted in Khmer.

So, what is your name?

My name is Ah Ya.

How old are you?

I am twenty-four. I was born in the Year of the Horse.

Yes. And where are you from?

I am from Svay Rieng Province.

When did you come to Phnom Penh?

Ten years ago, when I was fourteen.

Did you come alone?

No, with my family.

Do you still live with them?

Yes, I do.

Tell me about your family.

There are five children, all of us girls. Two are older than me and two are younger. My father has already died, but my mother is still alive.

I am sorry to hear about your father. How did he die?

He drank too much alcohol.

He suffered from liver failure?

No, he just went to sleep one night and never woke up. He had been drinking and went to sleep in his bed like usual. He just didn't wake up the next day.

I see. Have you ever studied English?

No, I haven't.

What languages can you speak?

Just Khmer. But I cannot read or write. Just speak.

I see. How long have you worked in a bar for?

Six months now... Wait [she calculated in her head] yes, six months.

So what did you do for the first nine years and six months you were here, in Phnom Penh?

I used to work in a house, for a family. I would cook, clean, wash the dishes and the clothes etc.

How much did you get paid there?

$40 per month.

$70 per month?

No, $40. $40 per month.

Wow! $40! That is very little! Did they provide you with food?

Yes, they did. Three meals a day

And how much do you earn here?

$105

Plus tips?

Yes, I get tips here. And lady drinks. Every time a customer buys me a drink the bar gives me $1.50.

Do you prefer here to cleaning?

Yes, I do. Here I can relax, there is no pressure. I don't have to wash or clean anything. I just sit and relax, and talk with customers and the other girls. The work is easy.

Does your family know you work here?

Yes, they do.

What do they think about it?

They think it is very bad. They think badly of me, but they understand [about the money]. Anyway, my mother has returned to our home province.

Do you go home with customers?

Yes, but not a lot. Just once or twice a month. Not much. It depends on how much I need the money. I have a family to support. And sometimes a customer would pay my $70 or $100 to go home with them. If I need the money, then I go.

Was your first time with a customer, or with a boyfriend?

With my husband.

You were married?

Yes, but we have broken up already.

Why was that?

He had another wife. He lied to me. He tried to keep it from me. But I saw her, I met her. I left him after that.

How old were you?

I was nineteen. He was forty-four.

He was a Khmer?

Yes, Khmer.

Did you have a child with him?

Yes, a little boy. He is two years old. He is at home in Svay Rieng, with my mother. I have to send money home every month. I want to stop working here, but I must support my family.

So you were twenty-two when you had him?

Yes. I fell pregnant at twenty-one. That is normal here, twenty-one is not considered too young to have a baby.

I see. Are you looking for a boyfriend here [in the bar]?

From where?

Well, up to you. The customers here are usually Australian or American or British...

Any except Khmer. I don't think I can love a Khmer again, after my marriage. He was unfaithful, and such a bad husband. And if I could find a better man, I wouldn't have to work.

I see. I think that is everything. Thank you very much for your time.

No problem. If any other girls want to speak with you I will call you.

That would be fantastic.

This interview was conducted in Phnom Penh, 28th March 2015.

I explained my motives to the interviewee and she agreed to answer any questions I may have.

Interview conducted in English.

What is your name?

My name is Sokh Lin. I am from Svay Reing province, near the Vietnam border.

Can you tell me about your family?

I have a daughter and I am pregnant. Look [Sokh Lin pulls her dress taut to expose a small bump]. But I am single now. My ex-boyfriend is a motherfucker. He works for the government, in the taxation department. It is a good job, he has a good salary. But he gambles, he gambles on sport on the internet. But he is bad at it. He has lost $80,000.

$80,000!? My goodness, that is so much!

Yes. I heard him talking with his friends. He never told me how much he earned, he never gave me any money. I asked for money for medicine for our little girl. She is just six! But he always said he didn't have the money, he couldn't buy the medicine. But he is always fucking girls from KTV, always fucking other girls. He is like a snake, you know?

I understand.

I hate it here. I have had such a hard life, such a sad life. It is impossible to make money in Cambodia. I have a friend from New Zealand, and he wanted to help me. He had a bar in Siem Reap and he wanted me to be the manager. But I was living here with my boyfriend, so he took another lady to be the manager. But she robbed him, took his motorbike and $3000 and left with her boyfriend. I should have gone, ha ha! But now he is in New Zealand. He offered to help me come to New Zealand. His friend is married to a Khmer, and she lives there too, so he knows about how to get a visa.

I see.

But he is sick now. He has cancer of the lungs and the liver. He will die soon. He has stopped replying to me, he cannot help. My chance to go and have a better life has gone. I am stuck here, fuck!

[The interview was paused for Sokh Lin to compose herself. Tissues were fetched]

Can I ask, what did you do before here? Your English is really very good.

I used to work for an NGO. But I never used to speak English. They used to speak in English and I couldn't understand. In the meetings I would just sit there, and think 'One day I want to be able to speak English'. But I couldn't afford formal lessons. After the NGO I worked in a factory, but I had a friend who studied

133

English. She would learn and then teach us. I would wake up at 05:00 and study English for two hours, before work started at 07:00. It was tiring, but now I can speak it. If I want something, I do it. I don't just wait.

I'm very impressed.

After the factory I worked in a pharmacy, selling creams. You know what I mean?

Yes, I do.

After that I came to bars. I am a cashier, but I can manage the business too. I used to work at another bar. I was on $250 a month, but it was hard. I had to manage the bar downstairs and the guesthouse upstairs. It was very difficult. But I was fired and came here.

Why were you fired?

The boss, the owner, wanted his brother to work there. He got rid of me so his brother could have a job. I was a good worker, but they are like that. Khmer always favour their friends and family, even if they are not very good.

I see. I have come across this before.

So here I am on only $150. And I have a child and I am pregnant and that shit doesn't help me!

[The interview was paused again for Sokh Lin to compose herself]

134

I mean, I would like to go home. Take my child home and live with my mother. But he knows where she lives, he knows my house in my province. I am so fucked... Thank you for listening to me. Really, thank you.

No, thank you. It has been painful for you to talk about these things.

It is ok. I am used to it. My whole life is sad. But I think this [this compilation] is a good idea. People think bar girls are bad, but we're not! I'm not a bad girl, not a slut. I have had a hard life and I work hard. People should know that.

Takeo

This interview was conducted in Phnom Penh, 14th April 2015.

I explained my motives to the interviewee and she agreed to answer any questions I may have.

Interview conducted in Khmer.

So, what is your name?

Everyone calls me Ming. [Ming means aunty in Khmer]

Ok Ming, can I ask, how old are you?

I am thirty-nine years old.

And where are you from? Which province?

Takeo province. It is very beautiful. *Ta* Mok was from Takeo.

Yes, I am familiar with Ta Mok. Can you tell me a bit about your family?

Ok, well, I have a mother and a father and I am one of eight children. There are four boys and four girls. And I have a son, from a previous marriage.

Wow, eight children! That is a lot! And how old is your son?

Yes, it is a big family! My son is 16 now. He goes to school.

What happened with your previous marriage?

I left him, in 2001. He was lazy. He did not work! I had to do everything; clean the house, care for him, care for our boy. And he did nothing. So I left. I am on my own, with my son, but I will get remarried in February [2016].

Is your new partner a Khmer? And does he know where you currently work?

Yes, he is a Khmer. He is a friend of my brother's. He doesn't know I work in a bar, of course not. None of my family do! I wouldn't want my son or parents to find out, they would be ashamed of me. I also worked in the market, so he thinks I just get my income from there.

Also? So you worked in the market at the same time as in the bar?

Yes. I have stopped now, now I know I will have a husband who can look after me. It was so tiring. I would work there, maybe 09:00 to 17:00, then cook for my son, then work here from 18:00 to 06:00, then get my son ready for school and do it all again.

Wow! Where did you sleep?

Well, I slept at the market. I have a chair there. And sometimes I can sleep here, a little bit. And if I go home with a customer, sometimes I can stay there.

So you go home with customers?

Sometimes. If I have no money, I have no money. If I have enough, then I don't need to.

Ok, I see. So, how long have you worked in bars?

Um, for around five months.

And do you like it here?

Not really. But I need the money. And working here is much better than when I worked in a factory! Here I have friends, and I can sit down and chat with them. And the pay is about the same as the factory.

How much is that?

$120 per month.

Ok, great. When you were younger, did you go to school? What languages can you speak?

I went to school when I was a child, but I never studied English. You had to pay extra to study English, and we didn't have the money. I only speak Khmer.

Ok, thanks. So, when you stop working here, what do you want to do?

I will get married, so I won't need to work. But I love to cook. Maybe I could do that, if I need to. But I'd rather not.

Ming, I think that is everything. Thank you very much, I think we have finished.

No problem.

This interview was conducted in Phnom Penh, 27th March 2015.

I explained my motives to the interviewee and she agreed to answer any questions I may have.

Interview conducted in English.

So, what is your name?

My name is Ah Dai. I am from Takeo Province. I am twenty-five years old. I have a mother, but my father has already died. My mum is still alive, and has a new, young husband.

Sorry, how did your father die?

He was shot. He was a policeman on Koh Kong [Island], and he was shot by a criminal. That was three years ago.

So, 2012?

Yes, in 2012. We had money then, but after he died we lost everything. We had no money after he died. I have only met my mother three times; once when I was twenty, then again when I was twenty-one, and the most recent time was two years ago, when I was twenty-three. I and my two brothers lived with our grandmother, as our father was away so much. She died when I was ten years old. She was dying for six months, and I had to care for her. I had to feed her, wash her, take her to the bathroom.

140

[There was a brief pause during which I left to fetch a box of tissues, for the interviewee was welling up]

Are you ok to go on?

Yes, I am. I don't need you to ask questions, I know what I want to say. Anyway, my mother still calls me...

But you don't actually meet her?

No, only ever a call. And only ever for money. And I told her, I will support her, if she needs medicine or something, but I refuse to give money to her husband. I want to study! I want to save up and go to school, not support him! I don't work to support him!

Do you live alone?

Yes, I rent. I live alone. I feel so old...

[Another brief pause for Ah Dai to compose her thoughts]

I go home with men, but not much. I used to have a boyfriend, from Sweden, but he is a dickhead. But he did pay for me to go to school. I lived with him in Kampong Som for two years. I borrowed money from him to open a restaurant. He finished with me because I couldn't speak English. But I can now... I am so unhappy. I work every day, from 5pm until 3am. I get two days off a month, but I work them too. I need the money. I must work every day. Without the tips I am fucked, you know? I am always number one for lady drinks, I always get the most. I need to. You know, many people ask my background. And I tell them, like I tell you now, but they think I am lying. Do you think I am lying?

No, I do not.

I am not lying. I fucking hate it. They think girls are useless. They think girls are just for fucking and cooking. I am so sad, I fucking hate this. Every day when I go to sleep, I lie awake and worry about the future. I am worried about who will look after me when I am old. I pray 'Why? I do good things. Why do you punish me?' I want to know why men aren't faithful... I see so many Khmer girls who marry foreigners and waste their money on clothes and smoking cigarettes. I just want money to eat! It isn't fair! I hate it!

[There was another brief pause whilst the interviewee composed her thoughts before continuing]

The foreigners ask me "How much are you? How much to go fuck?" and, if I like them, I say "I will give you a discount. Last time I charged $40, but for you I will charge $30" and they ask "Why are you so expensive?" This really makes me angry. I say "If you want a cheap girl, go to Wat Phnom! Get a girl from the street! And you will get HIV and they will rob you!"

I see.

The first two weeks here I was happy. I slept with just one guy, from Australia. I went with a friend. He had only been in Cambodia eight hours. He gave me and my friend $50 each. Some customers understand [pay well] and some don't... it is hard to find money. Some days I get just two or three dollars [in tips]. I used to celebrate my birthdays, but I don't anymore... I am a good person. If I see someone begging, I give them 1000R ($0.25) or 2000R ($0.50) because I don't want a bad life when I die [and am reincarnated]. I want a family in my next life... When I go to the pagoda I pray and ask 'Why don't you give me good luck?' Panha [page forty-six] helps me when I am sick. She is like a sister to me. No one else cares for me, I have no family...

When did you first come to Phnom Penh?

When my grandmother died [ten years ago]. I had never been here before. I stayed with a Khmer woman and her family. I had to do everything. I had to wash and clean everything. She didn't have a machine, you know, so I had to wash seven people's clothes by hand. She didn't pay me, she just gave me food, three meals a day. So I went to work in the bar. I worked for her for five years... I mean, I have wrist problems from all the work I had to do so young. But before I went to her I had nothing at all. Whenever I saw people wearing nice clothes or with a nice phone I would look and think 'I wish I could have that.'

What do you want to do when you leave here?

I want to open a restaurant. I am a good cook! I can cook all Khmer food, really well. But it is expensive... Here, I have no love. Love for money, love for fun, love for a short time. But I want love forever. Some girls here have sex for money and then waste it on alcohol and cigarettes. And then they have to go and fuck again. I just want to support my brothers.

Where are they? And how old are they?

They are in Takeo. One is twenty-six, the other twenty-eight.

What do they do?

The younger one is a cook for a family. The elder is a driver. I also have a big sister, but we have not met in many years, since I was very small. Maybe she is dead now, I don't know.

Do your brothers know you work here? In a bar?

No, they don't know. I have to be strong. I have no one to take care of me. All the girls who work in bars have problems. Maybe they had a bad Khmer husband or boyfriend, and want to try and find a western husband. Some girls are good, and some girls are bad, but all have problems.

I see

A customer almost killed me once. He tried to kill me. Would you like me to tell you?

Yes, if you don't mind.

One time I went home with this particular customer. He seemed nice. He had spent $1000 in the bar that night. He was close with another girl, but she was married. He didn't know this, and when he came to see her I told him that she was married, and had gone back to her home province with her husband to be with her family. He wanted to buy her a moto. I used to call him brother, I knew him well. But when I told him she was married he was upset, and drank a lot. I went back with him to a hotel, and he smoked in the toilet…

Sorry, what did he smoke? Cigarettes?

No, drugs. I am not sure. But it was drugs. He was in there a long time. He wanted to fuck me without a condom. I said no, and it made him angry. He beat me, he punched me, he punched my face. He threw my phone against the wall, breaking it. Then he put a knife to my throat. I began to cry. I told him 'Let me go. Let me go and I will not say anything. But if you kill me there will be big trouble. The police will come.' He threw me out, into the street, naked. I had just a towel. All my clothes were in the room. I told reception what had happened. I said 'There is a crazy man in room whatever. He fucked me and did not pay. He fucked me twice. He beat me, and wants to kill me. Tell the police.' Then I left.

I see. It must have been very frightening.

[She shrugs]

Yes, it was.

How many men have you slept with?

145

Not too many. I only go home once or twice a month. Sometimes I am cashier, sometime I make the drinks. I am skilled you know, I can speak English and I can count and I can mix drinks. Sometimes, when the manager is in Thailand, I manage the finances.

I see

Do you have anything else to ask?

No, I don't think I do. I would like to thank you for telling me this. It must have been hard to bring all this up.

Yes, it was. But it is the truth. It has all happened.

Thank you very much

This interview was conducted in Kampong Som, 28th March 2015.

I explained my motives to the interviewee and she agreed to answer any questions I may have.

Interview conducted in Khmer.

So, what is your name?

My name is Thida.

And where are you from Thida?

I am from Takeo Province. It is where Ta Mok came from. Do you know this man?

Yes, I know of him. He was very cruel.

Yes, he was. My village is twenty kilometres from his house. His house is now a police school, I think.

I see. So, you came from Takeo to work here, in Kampong Som?

Yes. Takeo is still poor. There are no jobs there. I and my brother both came here, to work here. He is a tuk tuk driver. But his English is poor, and most of the foreigners here only speak English. I can speak English every day because I work here. It is still not very good. But I will speak every day!

Do you have any other brothers or sisters?

Yes, two other sisters. I am the oldest, at twenty-three. My two younger sisters live with my mother and father. They are still in Takeo, studying. My brother and I save our money, and will take it back to Takeo with us. We help pay for the school fees. My mother and father have a shop, but they have little money.

So how long have you worked here in Kampong Som? And have you always worked in bars?

I have been here six months. We [her and her brother] came at the same time, and we live together. I started working in a restaurant, but then I changed to work in bars. If you are a pretty girl you don't need to be able to speak English to get tips. But if you cannot speak English in a restaurant it can cause problems. So I stopped there and came here.

Does your brother mind you working in a bar?

No, he doesn't mind. I don't go home with customers. He knows that. He works nights too so we sleep at the same time. He'd know if I did! He doesn't like it very much, but he knows it is the best job for me.

What do you mean?

The salary. I get $120 a month here, plus tips and lady drinks. So about $160 per month. I work ten hours a day, but the work is easy. I could work in a restaurant, carrying plates.

A waitress?

Yes, a waitress. The salary is the same but the work is hard and there are no tips.

I see.

When my sisters have finished school, I can stop working here. But the work is easy. Maybe I won't stop working here. The salary is ok. And sometimes I meet nice men here. Some men want me to be their girlfriend, but I know they will want sex. I am a virgin, I don't want this. Maybe I can find a nice boy who really loves me. And I can go back to his country. Work in England or America.

Thida, thank you for talking to me.

No problem. It has been nice speaking with you.

Printed in Great Britain
by Amazon